The New Sun

INTERSECTIONS

Asian and Pacific American
Transcultural Studies

Russell C. Leong
General Editor

The New Sun

新らしき太陽
八島太郎

Taro Yashima

University of Hawai'i Press
Honolulu

LIBRARY OF CONGRESS CATALOGING-IN-PUBLICATION DATA

Yashima, Taro, 1908-1994.

The new sun / Taro Yashima.

  p. cm. — (Intersections, Asian and Pacific American transcultural studies)

Originally published: New York : Henry Holt and Co., 1943.

ISBN 978-0-8248-3185-1 (cloth : alk. paper)

1. Yashima, Taro, 1908-1994. 2. Artists—Japan—Biography. I. Title.

NC1709.Y3A23 2008

741.6092—dc22

[B]

                              2008003094

University of Hawai'i Press books are printed on acid-free

 paper and meet the guidelines for permanence and durability of

the Council on Library Resources.

Printed by Versa Press

I thank the America which lets me talk
and write freely about people
and events which I shall never forget.
   —Taro Yashima

Foreword

One day about a year ago, Taro Yashima, a young Japanese artist, was brought into my office. I was at once impressed both by the character of his sketches and by his high integrity as an individual.

As a result of his unflinching opposition to the tide of militarism in Japan, he suffered grave persecutions. *The New Sun* was inspired by a deep desire to express graphically the story of his last years in Japan. Gradually it evolved into a vivid image of the tortures he endured and those endured by freedom-loving people throughout this war-torn world.

It has been a privilege to watch this book grow and to encourage Taro to complete it. Democratic Americans, I know, will appreciate the austere honesty of this human document.

Taro Yashima and his wife are happy and grateful to be living in America. His gifted brush is winning him many commissions in this country, but *The New Sun* ranks as a pure labor of love into which he has poured his full measure of devotion.

—Tobias Moss
New York
July, 1943

Contents

Introduction

NAOKO SHIBUSAWA

About ten years ago, as I leafed through dusty, bound copies of the *Saturday Review of Books* in my university's library, I happened on an unusual ad by the publishing house Henry Holt & Co. This ad, appearing in *Saturday Review*'s January 27, 1945 issue, promoted what Henry Holt called a "publishing failure."[1] The ad explained that a little over a year earlier, in late 1943, the publisher had released an autobiography by a Japanese political refugee and artist named Taro Yashima (1908–1994). The publisher confessed in the ad that it did not expect this sympathetic depiction of the enemy Japanese to become a best seller, but it published *The New Sun* because Yashima's struggle against Japanese imperialism and "for the simple dignities of the democratic way of life is one of the most moving evidences of man's incalculably slow progress in this weary world." Hoping that *The New Sun* would attract the attention of "opinion-moulders" as well as of "men and women of good will," the publisher gave away seven hundred advance copies, "not only to [its] regular reviewers but to liberals in every walk of life—art, government, politics." Despite excellent reviews—the *New York Times* called *The New Sun* a "simple and moving document" told with "economy and eloquence"— the overall response to the book was disappointingly tepid.[2] One publicity man, who thought so highly of Yashima's book that he promoted the book without charge, "was baffled when he got nowhere."[3] Henry Holt's salesmen reported, "Nobody will buy a book from a Jap."

Trying to market the book once more to a select audience in January 1945, Henry Holt advertised it in the *Saturday Review of Books*, a newsprint magazine that published book reviews and articles by academics, public intellectuals, and writers—much like the *New York Review of Books* today. The *Saturday Review* ceased publication in 1982, but during its heyday at mid-century, it represented the progressive edge of the liberal consensus. While critical of U.S. policy, the writers in the *Saturday Review* still tended to see U.S. geopolitical objectives and the cause of freedom and liberty as basically one and the same. Convinced that the declared policy goals of the United States involving political freedom should not remain hollow to millions, the *Saturday Review* insisted that Euroamericans needed to be tolerant of nonwhites, both at home and abroad. The magazine was an early advocate of civil rights and featured the works of minority writers, including Filipino Carlos Bulosan, whose image graced the cover of the March 9, 1946 issue.[4]

Appealing, therefore, to the *Saturday Review*'s intellectual elite, liberal readership, Henry Holt emphasized in its ad that it considered the book a failure "not because it lost us a few thousand dollars but because, as far as we know, it has supplied no yeast for the American mind." Like most books on Japan published in wartime America, *The New Sun* censures Japanese militarism, but unlike them, it sharply criticizes it from a Japanese perspective. That Americans were uninterested in this perspective—that Americans could not see beyond wartime racism—was a "disheartening" indicator, Henry Holt bemoaned, about their nation's ability to lead "the rest of the world" in the postwar years to come. Urging the *Saturday Review*'s readership to rethink their notions of the Japanese, the ad's final line noted that Yashima was currently somewhere at sea, working for the U.S. Navy, "still drawing pictures against his enemies."

I came across this ad while researching postwar American discourse on the former Japanese enemy. Although the name Taro Yashima sounded vaguely familiar, I had never heard of *The New Sun*. I was surprised that a mainstream American publisher not only printed but also actively supported, at an apparent financial loss, a sympathetic portrayal of the Japanese—first in 1943, when the worst fighting in the Pacific was yet to come, and again in January 1945, before conventional and atomic bombs pummeled most Japanese cities into rubble. This was exceptional, for virtually absent in wartime America were depictions of the "good Japanese" who were opposed to the policies of Imperial Japan, such as the kind offered by *The New Sun*. Most Americans during the war appeared to succumb to a pervasive racialized hatred of the Japanese. Even liberals like Theodor Geisel (a.k.a.

Dr. Seuss) relied on racist, "Jap" stereotypes in his wartime cartoons.[5] While Americans talked of "good Germans" who resisted the Nazi regime, they usually presented the Japanese as an undifferentiated mass that mindlessly obeyed the dictates of their so-called god-emperor. The Japanese were seen, as a wartime propaganda film infamously put it, like "prints off the same photographic negative."[6] In other words, most Americans did not believe—nor did they want to believe—that a Japanese counterpart to the "good German" existed. The notion that Asians lacked individuality, manly backbone, and the capacity for positive initiative was deeply entrenched in American popular culture and, as Henry Holt discovered, almost impossible to dislodge. Most Americans resisted the idea of Japanese resistance; they were unprepared or unwilling to consider the idea of the "good Japanese" in 1943 and 1944.

Intrigued by the ad, I immediately checked the computer database to see if a copy of Yashima's book was available in the library. It was, and I walked over to the appropriate stacks and found it. The volume was an unassuming hardcover with dark blue binding. When I opened it, I was stunned. *The New Sun* turned out to be a graphic autobiography—like Miné Okubo's graphic memoir of the Japanese American internment, *Citizen 13660* (1946). As in other graphic novels about World War II, such as Keiji Nakagawa's *Hadashi no Gen* [*Barefoot Gen*] (originally serialized 1973, 1974) and Art Spiegelman's *Maus* (originally serialized 1972), the illustrations take precedence over the text. But instead of the sharper, clearer lines of these three other works, Yashima's art combines Japanese brush technique with Western pen and ink. As a result, it is more roughly drawn, showing a postimpressionist influence and making effective use of shadow and light. This chiaroscuro effect superbly dramatizes moments of oppression, confusion, and despair, as well as hope and optimism in his story. At the same time, he flawlessly integrates elements of caricature to provide devastating portraits of the unsavory characters in his tale. The quality of his art and the economy of the text make *The New Sun* a powerful and riveting tale of political dissidence against Japanese imperialism. I checked the back inside cover and saw that the book had not been checked out in decades. As I read Yashima's moving and gripping story, I became convinced that I held in my hands a largely forgotten gem.[7]

The New Sun telescopes back and forth in time, with Yashima using a narrative device to tell a story within a story. He begins in the spring of 1933, just after he, his wife, and toddler son move into a "sunny house" in a poor working-class neighborhood. Describing how they busily settled into their new home—planting a garden, befriending neighbors, working as freelance artists as their son attended a neighborhood nursery—Yashima opens his tale with a happy moment in their lives. Readers soon discover, however, that this was a small ray of sunshine surrounded by a darker world that soon closes in on them. The first sign of this darkness is the sudden closing of the nursery by the order of the *tokkōka*, a division of the thought control police.[8] Then, tragically, their toddler unexpectedly dies of a mysterious ailment. One evening soon thereafter, Yashima comes home to find his wife gone and strange men in his house. They take him away without a word, offer no justification, and slap him when he asks for an explanation. These men, of course, are the *tokkōka*, and they escort him to a prison, where his wife is already locked up in the women's section.

There, at the prison, Yashima and his wife languish for months on end without knowing when they might be released. With the other prisoners they endure poor food, dreadful tedium, sleep deprivation, and the petty whims of guards who torment them for amusement. Sometimes, their small cells—only six feet by six feet—become so crowded that prisoners must sleep sitting up.[9] Appeals from family and friends on their behalf for clemency are futile. There is particular concern for Yashima's wife, who discovered that she was pregnant again shortly before her arrest. But, as Yashima relates, the *tokkōka* are unmoved; they even arrest their family doctor after he comes to the prison to plead for her release. This arbitrary system of justice metes out harsh punishment for other trivial offenses. One fellow inmate in Yashima's cell is a newsboy who had been arrested for peeping through a hole in a factory wall. Another is a Korean garbage man who tried to steal one zinc pipe. "As he said," Yashima remarks, "this was nothing compared to Japan's seizure of all Korea."

Months later, Yashima and his wife are both finally called in front of the thought police chief, who bullies and taunts them. At the end of his interrogation, he orders them to write a "personal history." Although it is not completely clear in Yashima's narrative, the chief was probably not asking for a genuine personal history, but demanding a *tenkō* statement—a statement of repudiation. The thought police forced political prisoners to compose and sign such statements to renounce political associations and beliefs. These *tenkō* statements were then used to weaken the resolve of other imprisoned or newly arrested associates. But rather than writing the "personal history" expected by the *tokkōka*, Yashima produces a more faithful account of his childhood and earlier years of political activism, which he unfolds for us, his readers.

He was born, he writes, as the younger son of a village doctor who, by example and words, stressed humanitarianism and a social obligation to heal others. In addition to treating the sick and injured of their village, his father gave medical attention wherever he chanced upon people needing it. "The peoples of the world are brothers," his father often repeated. "Doctors are made for humanity." Yashima's childhood friends were farmers' children who were "geniuses" at small handicrafts. After they graduated from their village school, Yashima says he went on to high school in a nearby city, but his friends began working full-time and their formal education stopped. After high school, Yashima matriculated into the Imperial Art Academy in Tokyo. Despite this enormous privilege, Yashima explains that he found higher education rigid, uninspiring, and militarized. Meanwhile, on visits back to his village, he saw old friends looking gloomy and farmers grumbling that students "didn't even know the price of rice." On later visits, he remembered finding that infant mortality had increased and that farmers were unfairly being saddled with debt. The poorest ones had lost their fields and had migrated to earn a living elsewhere. Most disturbingly, the farmers—as well as urban workers—struggling to eke out a living were being pounded with a message to go to war for the "Peace of the East." It made no sense, Yashima recalls. "Whose peace on earth would it be when that peace was made by forcing working people to use their hands to kill other working people?"

Subsequently expelled from the art academy, he claims, for missing a military drill and insubordination, Yashima joined like-minded artist friends in "an art movement [that] had a progressive philosophy." Giving up a future as a high school teacher with a comfortable apartment provided by the state, Yashima explains that he came to believe that artists, too, had a social obligation to "humanity." More politicized than his doctor-father, he felt that artists had a duty to understand and bring greater awareness about the struggles of ordinary people. Yashima describes how he, his new wife— another artist in the movement—and their cohorts lived among farmers, talked to the urban unemployed, and put on a well-attended "people's art exhibition," which included work that ridiculed militarists. The artists also sent their exhibit on tour and got reproductions of their art printed in magazines to spread their anti-imperialist message. The artists believed that they should and could, through their art, extract a power deep within the people to "stop the militarism, the oppression, the fascism of [the] time."

This antimilitarist movement protested what they called "the war of aggression in China," and it was "active," Yashima recounts, in "every field—law, medicine, music, motion pictures, literature, and drama." But in 1931, Yashima explains, "the storm which broke over Manchuria, destroying the freedom of the Manchurian and Chinese people, also began to blow through the islands of Japan." That year, the Japanese Imperial Army invaded China and subjugated Manchuria, which became the Japanese puppet state of Manchukuo. In Yashima's recollections, it was then that the Japanese government also began stamping out domestic dissent and exacting greater obedience from its own citizenry. The exhibits were dismantled; the periodicals that previously printed their work now rejected them; the artists who had regular jobs began to lose them; and speakers were arrested for merely saying the word *oppression*. To drum up support for Imperial Japan's aggressive policies, the Japanese magazines resorted to fear-mongering and cast the war as a defensive one against "terrorism." Meanwhile, their progressive organization weakened as experienced leaders were arrested and replaced by less skillful ones. Dissatisfied also with the "mock intellectuals" who were beginning to populate their group, Yashima and his wife moved to another part of the city, to live among the working class. Bringing us to the point where he began *The New Sun*, Yashima then explains that he ended his "personal history" for the *tokkōka* with a defiant statement about how nothing could "stifle" the culture of dissent. His spirit obviously not yet broken, Yashima waited for the consequence.

This turned out to be a beating so severe that he was knocked into unconsciousness. A few days afterward, he was forced to join his district's army reserves. In this depiction, Yashima both mocks and condemns the cruel and bombastic drill officers as delusional, and then contrasts them to the essential humanity and emergent solidarity he finds among his cellmates back in the prison. The prisoners always give the best part of their lunch to the one who had been tortured and beaten to show sympathy; freed prisoners invariably leave behind an article of clothing as a token of thanks to the others in the prison cell; the prisoners learn to communicate secretly and clandestinely pass along reading materials; once, a sushi seller tries t. raise the spirits of his cellmates by pretending to make and serve sushi made of handkerchiefs; and another time, the male prisoners successfully lobby to get a bottle of milk to a trolley car union organizer who had fallen gravely ill due to malnutrition. This act of generosity and caring—coming from men who were starving themselves—so moves the organizer that he cannot sleep, and Yashima remembers finding him writing a poem on the prison wall in the middle of the night. Yet, as he also shows, among the prisoners were turncoats who became informants for better treatment and early release.

In the end, Yashima decides to give the thought police the statement they desired in order to be freed from prison.[10] He explains his decision as a pragmatic one, as "a new reality" set upon him. He thought about the various people he had encountered: the poor farmer who hungered to buy books; the boy who hated his alcoholic father and dreamt of being a sign painter to help his hardworking mother; the farmer who became "strangely quiet and unlike himself after he had killed a pleading mother and child in Manchuria"; the Korean children who scavenged for tin in junkyards; the dock worker who tried signing with a German sailor to find out about conditions in Germany; and so on. Knowing that all these fundamentally decent people were being propagandized to kill other Asians, Yashima becomes convinced that he could be of more use outside of prison rather than inside it, powerless to effect any change.

Perhaps most significantly, though he does not explicitly say this, he is motivated to capitulate by worries about his wife and their unborn child. One of the most poignant descriptions in *The New Sun* is Yashima hearing the screams of his pregnant wife being beaten. The sounds are agonizing. Here again, he may lose yet another baby—and even more important, his wife—but he is helpless, unable to protect either of them. Fortunately, mother and unborn baby survive the beating, but she remained imprisoned until her ninth month of pregnancy.[11] Through his prison window he sees her leaving, heavy with child. But since the prisoners are denied outside news, he does not know whether their child was born alive, or if his wife, given her weakened condition, survived labor and delivery. Upon his release from prison, his discovery that his wife had given birth to another baby boy and that both were in good health ends the book on an ambivalently optimistic note. Freed from the cramped prison cell and traveling to his wife and new

sun shining upon him. "Surely this new sun"—quite unlike
zed by the flag of Imperial Japan, he implies—"would
tness over me and over all people everywhere."

Yashima dedicated the book to his new home: "I thank
..ca, ne wrote, "which lets me talk and write freely about people
and events [that] I shall never forget." By this time, he and his wife were
unofficial political refugees in the United States. Just as *The New Sun*
described, both had been arrested several times for their artwork opposing
Japanese imperialism and fascism.[12] In Japan, they were known as Iwamatsu
Jun and Iwamatsu Tomoe (nee Sasako Tomoe).[13] Iwamatsu Tomoe was an
artist in her own right. Iwamatsu/Yashima later recalled being arrested at
least ten times between 1928 and 1933 and estimated that he must have
spent a total of over three years in prison. In 1939, the couple decided to leave
Japan for their own safety and so that Jun could avoid being drafted into
the Japanese Imperial Army. A friend of Tomoe's father owned a shipping
company and offered free fare abroad one of his freighters if they could pay
for their meals. A relative helped get them passports, and they went to
New York on a tourist visa, leaving their four-year-old son, Makoto, in his
maternal grandparents' care.[14] In February 1941, the Iwamatsus changed
their visa status from visitors to students, a status change justified by their
continuing study of art in New York City. After the war began, they elected
to stay in the United States rather than being repatriated back to Japan on
the *Gripsholm* in the summer of 1942.[15]

After war between Japan and the United States commenced, Tomoe fell
into a depression, sick with worry knowing—as she later put it—that the
"best guns" would now be facing her son.[16] Jun, however, threw his energies
into drawing satirical cartoons of Japanese leaders, just as he had done in
prewar Japan. He sought to use his talents for U.S. war propaganda because
he desired a quick American victory. Continuing to believe that Imperial
Japan's war effort was morally wrong, he now saw it as doomed, and he
wanted as many Japanese lives as possible to be spared. After all, the rural
youth who were similar to his childhood friends made up the majority of
the Japanese military forces. After making rounds at magazine publishers
in New York City with his portfolio, he finally met an editor who trusted
his sincerity in wanting a U.S. victory, and this editor put him in touch
with Tobias Moss, art director of the Office of War Information (OWI).
"I've been waiting for someone like you," said Moss upon meeting Jun, the

Japanese man later recalled.[17] Moss put him to work at the OWI, and the Iwamatsus decided to use a pseudonym to protect their young son left in Japan.[18] They became Taro and Mitsu Yashima, pseudonyms they used as their professional names for the rest of their lives.

With Moss's approval, he stopped working for the OWI in 1943 to write and illustrate *The New Sun*—a task he was able to do with support from a variety of friends, both Americans and other Japanese who chose to remain in the United States. Their landlord—a kindly, white-haired old man named Cooper—even allowed the Iwamatsus to live rent-free so that he would be able to finish the book.[19]

Iwamatsu/Yashima's gratitude toward those in his new home was thus heartfelt, and it made him a very unusual Issei—and I call him an Issei because he ended up living out almost the rest of his life in the United States and because his children, grandchildren, and great-grandchildren are U.S. citizens.[20] A political refugee unlike most Japanese immigrants, he also was thanking the United States in 1943, at a time when most Japanese immigrants had become political prisoners, locked up by the U.S. government. Essentially dispossessed of their homes and businesses, most Issei did not see the United States as a "new sun" of democracy as Yashima seemed to say it was. But if we look at the wording of the dedication carefully, Yashima says he thanks "*the* America which" allows him his freedoms. He was not thanking Americans or the United States wholesale, but the part of the United States that still preserved and valued civil liberties, even for "enemy aliens." Yashima was, of course, aware of the internment. Decades later, he remembered that the attack on Pearl Harbor threw the Nikkei in America overnight to "the bottom of hell," but his 1943 work does not mention what he later called their "forced migration to the desert."[21] *The New Sun* therefore does not indict the American public for the racist policy of its government, but rather, it reminded them of their nation's nobler ideals. In this respect, Yashima's book was similar to Bulosan's 1946 autobiographical account. Both *The New Sun* and *America Is in the Heart* were antiracist pleas targeted toward a liberal, Euroamerican audience that emphasized the humanity and suffering of the Japanese and Filipino peoples.[22] But of course, since the Japanese themselves also caused so much suffering, most Americans were not prepared to feel kindly toward them. The Japanese rural boys that Yashima remembered so fondly, like other rural and urban boys throughout the world, committed horrific atrocities when they became wartime soldiers away from home. Seen in this light, it is little wonder that *The New Sun* did not sell well during the war.[23] For the reading public, rather than owning up to a common humanity and a common inhumanity, it was and continues to be much easier to regard the enemy as something other—as egregious, capable of depravities unimaginable by one's own soldiers.

But however reluctant Americans were to acknowledge the existence of "good Japanese" during the war, they became much more willing to do so afterward. This was not simply a matter of letting bygones be bygones, but a shift that dovetailed with U.S. policy to promote their former enemy as the "bulwark against communism" and America's most important ally in Asia. The "Jap" enemy consequently became a valuable, "junior ally" in American public discourse. While this turnabout appeared sudden, it had its origins in prewar conceptions of Japan as well as in wartime U.S. government programs—especially the national character studies sponsored by the Foreign Morale Analysis Division (FMAD) of the OWI and U.S. psychological warfare (psywar) in the Southwest Pacific. Unlike those trying to strengthen the U.S. homefront morale with racist stereotypes of the enemy, the national character scholars and the psywar personnel sought to understand the Japanese on a more sophisticated level that humanized them, rather than seeing them as suicidal fanatics.[24] Henry Holt's sponsorship of Yashima's book was thus a preview, though perhaps a premature one, of how American periodicals, books, films, and charity initiatives re-imagined the Japanese after the war—by imagining "the people" as distinct from the Japanese "militarists" who led them into war.[25]

The U.S. government did not orchestrate the postwar effort to remake the Japanese in the American public's imagination, but it does appear that the OWI had a role in publishing Yashima's book. Yashima's OWI supervisor, Tobias Moss, not only helped him secure the book contract for *The New Sun*, but also wrote its preface and had it translated into Japanese and, Moss claimed, "distributed into Nisei areas." (Moss proved to be an important contact. He not only championed *The New Sun*, but he also used the OWI's authority to recommend freelancing opportunities for Yashima during the war in *Fortune* and *Vogue*.)[26] So it may be that U.S. state support was the reason why the publisher could give away seven hundred copies during the war when paper was being rationed.

The New Sun therefore had multiple political uses: in Japanese, to convince the Issei (not Nisei who could, of course, read the original English version) of the political repression in Japan and, in English, to try to humanize the Japanese to an American audience. Later, *The New Sun* served as an edifying text in Occupation Japan—for it was translated and printed in Japan in 1949.[27] Yashima, then, not only helped create in print but also modeled in real life the "freedom-loving" Japanese that later became appreciated by the U.S. government and liberal Americans as a valuable Cold War ally.

After finishing *The New Sun*, Yashima did not return to the OWI but began work for the Office of Strategic Services (OSS) in August 1944. As the Henry Holt ad stated, he was overseas in January 1945. Stationed in the China-Burma-India Theater in the Morale Operations of the OSS, he participated in the U.S. war effort against his native country by composing and drawing propaganda leaflets that urged his countrymen to surrender and cease fighting. In November 1944, his wife also joined the OSS, but remained stateside.[28] Since her duties included making radio broadcasts, she was, in a sense, like an American counterpart to the so-called Tokyo Rose. But unlike Iva Toguri d'Aquino, the unfortunate Nisei woman ensnared by the mythic name and reputation, Tomoe Iwamatsu/Mitsu Yashima purposefully tried to weaken the resolve of her fellow Japanese in continuing the fight.[29] Both husband and wife, along with other Japanese and Japanese Americans with Japanese-language skills, translated Japanese documents, created propaganda, and brainstormed with their American superiors about the most effective way to make Japanese soldiers surrender rather than fighting to the death.

Although they worked toward U.S. victory, the Japanese collaborators and the Nisei personnel were seen as security risks by the OSS. Most of the Nisei personnel were Kibei, those Nisei who returned to the United States after spending some years in Japan. The Kibei had the necessary Japanese-language skills, unlike most of their fellow Nisei. Considered to have more intimate knowledge and presumably greater sympathy for Japan, the Kibei were deemed particularly untrustworthy by the U.S. military. As the OSS personnel file of a Kibei hired with Jun Iwamatsu/Taro Yashima noted: "Subject would be ordinarily Security Disapproved, and the possible dangers attendant on his employment are fully known to this office as well as to the branch heads." Limited security clearance was given, however, owing to the dearth of personnel with the required language skills. The OSS supervisors saw the danger as twofold: the Japanese/Nisei agent might betray the United States, and the Japanese/Nisei agent might be mistaken for and killed as an enemy. To prevent either occurrence, the OSS took strict measures to supervise Japanese/Nisei agents' work and to ensure, understandably, that all their work in the United States and abroad "be done in properly secured areas."[30]

After the war, Jun Iwamatsu went back to Japan wearing the uniform of a U.S. soldier. As part of the Strategic Bombing Survey, he mostly interviewed atomic bomb survivors in Nagasaki. In the Kobe home of his in-laws, he enjoyed a reunion with his son, Mako, whom he had not seen in over six years. But he chose not to visit his hometown, Nejime, in Kagoshima Prefecture. When he telephoned an old, favorite teacher, he learned that those familiar with his political artwork had not been fooled by his pseudonym and resented him, especially in small, close-knit Nejime. Out of concern for Iwamatsu, this teacher advised him not to come home, yet, because he would face tremendous hostility.[31] As he no longer had immediate family living in Nejime, he stayed away and remained largely anonymous in other places and in large cities such as Kobe. Yet his American uniform must have surely raised eyebrows. Probably causing even more suspicion was the fact that he spoke perfect Japanese, which marked him as native-born and bred, unlike the Nisei, those other U.S. servicemen with Japanese faces.

Whether or not they believed the Greater East Asian War was justified or even wise policy, all Japanese in the home islands had been suffering tremendously. Except for Kyoto, large swathes of all major cities and smaller towns had been reduced to ashes, and the population was starving. They knew that their compatriots overseas in Asia had endured greater deprivations and hardships, most especially the Japanese soldiers who had fought hopelessly in order to protect them in the home islands. The healthy, well-fed Iwamatsu, then, appeared to have not only escaped this national collective suffering, but also abetted the very enemy that caused their agonies. Even decades later, after a long period of U.S.-Japanese amity, some Japanese would react to Iwamatsu's wartime story with surprise and some resentment.[32] Such a response could also be found stateside among the Issei. Raised in Japan during an era of nationalistic chauvinism and resentful of the racism they encountered in the United States, a number of Issei took pride in Japan's early military victories and considered the United States as "the enemy."[33] Iwamatsu was deeply disturbed by these views of him as a traitor—that they refused to understand that he tried to save Japanese lives;

that they could not see that ending Japanese imperialism would usher in "a new democratic age" in Japan.

During the war, Iwamatsu/Yashima began work on a sequel to *The New Sun*, another graphic autobiography that attempts to explain why he left Japan. Whereas *The New Sun* contains only English text, this new book, *Horizon Is Calling*—published in 1947, also by Henry Holt—has both English and Japanese text on each page. Again, the English text helps to humanize the Japanese to an American audience, but the Japanese text indicates that the author had a different purpose for the Japanese and Issei audience who could read it. And though he explains why he left Japan, Yashima is not apologetic; he does not make excuses for himself. In this newer book, he takes up the story where he left it at the end of *The New Sun*. He is now out of prison, living with his wife's family, and trying to develop further as an artist. Seeing Makoto growing into a spunky yet knowing toddler is clearly the joy of his life. But Yashima depicts a larger, oppressive darkness shrouding the family: his father-in-law has been forced to sell his shipyard to militarists; his older sister-in-law mourns for her college days in the United States; and his young school-age brother is punished by his teachers for questioning the war. Conditions are worse for poorer Japanese such as his old friend, Kenji, a gentle, wise soul who is drafted into the Imperial Army. Most everyone, Yashima implies, even the battalion commander at Kenji's induction site, understands the war is a lost cause and suicidal. At the very end of the book, Yashima is resigned that he, too, will soon receive his draft papers. To prepare for this forced separation from his family and his uncertain end, he goes to a peninsula near his native village to draw scenic paintings that can be sold to support his wife and son after his departure. But as he gazes at and paints the wide expanse of the ocean, a "dream" of a different fate comes to him. Seeing himself in a museum overseas, studying the actual works of the great masters, he thinks of "escaping" Japan. The horizon, then, appears to be beckoning him to affirm life and to realize that his life's work is not yet over.

As in his first book, *Horizon Is Calling* ends on an ambivalent note. At the time it was published, the Yashima/Iwamatsus' fate was still uncertain. After briefly serving in the Occupation, Iwamatsu left Japan to return to the United States. Once again, he had to leave Mako behind because the Japanese exclusion provision of the 1924 Immigration Act forbade his son's entry into the United States. In the service of the U.S. Armed Forces,

Iwamatsu of course had special dispensation. Upon his return to New York in 1946, Iwamatsu and his wife began a legal battle to bring their son to the United States as well as to fight their own deportation, their student visas having expired years earlier. News of their effort was brought to the attention of the *New York Times*, prompting a June 1, 1946 editorial that asserted that Japanese aliens who served the United States during the war—especially Jun Iwamatsu—should not be repaid for "services rendered" by being deported.[34] Since it was too grand an effort to revise the immigration law, the Iwamatsus sought passage of a private law that would allow them to be an exception to the 1924 Immigration Act. Former OSS officers and others wrote on behalf of Jun Iwamatsu, and a year later, a bill for the private law was brought before Congress for consideration. Congressional subcommittee members, especially Senator Pat McCarran, initially opposed it. "These aliens have no roots in this country . . . . And there is an indication in the file both Iwamatsu and his wife have Communist leanings," McCarran asserted.

This, in fact, was true. In Japan, both Jun and Tomoe Iwamatsu had been members of the left-wing Proletariat Artists League which, as with Proletariat Artists Leagues in other countries, had close ties with the Communist Party. In New York, they remained active in circles of leftist expatriate Japanese.[35] But after the war, with a new Cold War intensifying, the Iwamatsus' supporters had to minimize these associations in order to prevent their deportation. A former associate of Jun—a specialist in Asian art at the Smithsonian—thus challenged McCarran's charge. He explained that the Japanese Consulate in New York "used to go around saying to all and sundry that Jun Iwamatsu was a communist, but as officials of the Imperial Government, that was part of their job." This Asianist insisted, however, that "Jun Iwamatsu is an artist first and foremost, and as such he has a certain innate, stubborn simplicity and truth in him, which can brook no tyranny. That is what got him into trouble with the Thought Control Police." Citing his own experiences in Japan, the Asianist continued, "I have seen and talked with Japanese Communists and I think I know the type. Jun Iwamatsu has not the faintest breath of that atmosphere about him." Likewise, a former OSS associate asserted, "I could not support this bill if these people were Communists. . . . No such tendencies were shown, and on the contrary the Iwamatsus were shown to be completely loyal to the United States and the principles for which it stands." It was also important, argued yet another former OSS agent, "that we, as a great nation, be generous in our appreciation of those of minority races within our midst who proved their loyalty under fire."[36]

McCarran later relented. The former OSS agent's reasoning that the United States needed to demonstrate charity and tolerance toward "the minority races" spoke to concerns about domestic race relations, as well as the geopolitical struggle against communism in an era of postcolonial revolutions. Working, therefore, in the Iwamatsus' favor were the same "Cold War civil rights" that prompted the U.S. federal government, now concerned about its image as the "leader of the free world," to throw its support toward ending legal and extralegal discrimination against racial minorities.[37] The Iwamatsus also happened to have the *New York Times* and well-connected individuals supporting their case, including OSS founder William "Wild Bill" Donovan. Trying to convince another senator to drop his opposition to Iwamatsu, McCarran emphasized, "If Bill Donovan says this man is all right, he is all right."[38] Later embracing the spirit of Cold War civil rights, McCarran coauthored the bill that became the McCarran-Walter Act (1952), which legalized once more Japanese immigration to the United States on a strict quota basis. The law was a symbolic gesture to demonstrate the goodwill of the United States to the Japanese at the end of Occupation.[39] The Iwamatsus, however, did not have to wait that long. On June 29, 1948, the 80th Congress passed Private Law 400, which allowed Makoto Iwamatsu to immigrate to the United States and his parents to remain stateside.[40] Red-tape bureaucracy delayed Makoto's arrival in the United States, and he was able to finally join his parents and meet his new baby sister a year later. The Iwamatsu family luckily avoided deportation and were able to overcome the state barriers to their family reunion. In contrast, many other Japanese American families during this immediate postwar period continued to be separated from family members "stranded" in Japan since before the war.

Both Jun and Tomoe Iwamatsu had been leading members of the Japan Proletariat Artists League, but in their new lives in the United States after the war—and during the McCarthy era—they left behind their activist past, Jun apparently forever and Tomoe until the 1960s. They moved to Los Angeles in 1954, and as Taro and Mitsu Yashima, they concentrated on their art, which became decidedly less political. After suffering from ulcers for several years, Yashima began writing children's books around the time they moved to California because he wanted to tell his American-born daughter, Momo, about life in his native land. He opened the Yashima Institute of Art, but became most famous as a Caldecott Honor–winning author of gentle, evocative picture books for young children. As a reviewer of his first children's book observed, "The work of Taro Yashima leaves [one] with a strong feeling that here is an artist-writer who knows children, respects and loves them deeply."[41]

As an earnest youth, Yashima had believed that "the artist belongs to the people"—that artists had a responsibility to interpret and depict the "reality" of hardworking people in order to bring about political change to improve and protect lives. By the mid-1950s, his philosophy and strategy had changed. "Let children enjoy living on this earth, let children be strong enough not to be beaten or twisted by evil on this earth," he advised fellow authors of children's books.[42] He now depicted "reality" from a child's sense of wonder and curiosity, especially in *The Village Tree* (1953), *Plenty to See* (1954, coauthored with his wife), and *Umbrella* (1958). The children in his books are not always innocent; at times they are capable of cruelty. His best-known book, *The Crow Boy* (1956), about a small, timid boy teased and ignored by his classmates, is a plea for understanding and multicultural sensitivity.[43] These were picture books that I loved as a child—which was why the name Taro Yashima had sounded so familiar when I first read the Henry Holt ad. I see now, although it is much more subdued, that Yashima's political idealism is visible in his later works of children's literature.

In contrast, Mitsu retained an activist ideal. She spent the 1950s raising Momo and practicing her art, but by the time Momo was a teenager, Mitsu was an antiwar and civil rights activist. Momo recalls how her mother took her and her high school friend to many rallies to protest the Vietnam War. Once, at her mother's prompting, Momo and her friend attended a meeting that featured a speech by Coretta Scott King. Soon after Momo left the house for college, Mitsu left Taro. There had been another woman for over a decade.[44] It is unclear if Mitsu finally felt free to leave Taro after Momo left the house; if cordial relations could not be maintained without Momo as their conduit; or if it was a combination of these and some other unknown factors. What is known is that Mitsu Yashima moved to San Francisco and blossomed as an artist and activist, no longer in her husband's shadow. She became a force among Bay Area Asian American artists, continued her antiwar activism, and even participated in the Native American occupation of Alcatraz Island during 1969–1970.[45] For reasons that may be attributed to her positionality as a woman and perhaps to her temperament, Mitsu kept a sense of urgency about striving for a more just world throughout her life.

The war and its aftermath, in contrast, deeply and negatively affected Taro for years thereafter. His wartime collaboration with the United States made him a traitor to the Imperial Japanese state, he knew, but not to the Japanese people, he hoped. The narratives he produced during the war—both for the U.S. government and for a U.S. publishing house—were not only meant to speed the war's end, but also to challenge American caricatures of the bucktoothed, myopic "Jap." As he later explained, the concept of *The New Sun* began with his conviction that the Japanese people were not naturally war-mongering and that Japanese militarism had a devastating effect on the Japanese also.[46] In his prewar activities opposing Japanese imperialism and militarism, he tried to persuade his fellow Japanese to recognize this about themselves, and in his wartime cooperation with the United States, he strived to convince Americans and Japanese of their mutual humanity.

Japanese historian Sodei Rinjirō posited decades later that Yashima took the risk to "transcend national boundaries" for this larger humanitarian goal.[47] Yashima's story, however, shows how difficult it was to do this: however much an individual tried to rise above national boundaries, legal restrictions and external demands for loyalty to a single state usually prevented such transcendence. Due to his skills, Yashima was valued and appreciated by the U.S. state and found a political haven in his new home; yet he retained feelings of allegiance to his country of birth and to its people. His transnational story reminds us that even if border-crossing individuals ascribed to widespread, "universal" aspirations for justice, humane treatment, and peace, they were not necessarily free from the power of nationalism. This nationalism came not only from the state but also from the historical actors themselves—from their abiding and deep sense of kinship with and loyalty to a particular group of people on land sacred to them.[48]

If we just look at the American side of Taro Yashima's story, it appears to be a traditional one of immigrant success. He escaped the political tyranny of the homeland and became an established and respected artist in his new home. By opting not to "rock the boat" in his new home, he can even be interpreted, in hindsight, as representing a "model minority." His children thrived in the United States, and all four grandchildren attended elite universities—including two in the Ivy League. His son not only survived the prenatal beatings endured by his mother and eventually joined his parents in the United States, but also became a well-known, Oscar- and Tony-nominated actor who went by the stage name Mako. Mako played the evil emperor opposite California's current governor in the *Conan the Barbarian* series, and in 2002, he was in *Pearl Harbor*, playing Admiral Isoroku Yamamoto, the mastermind of the Pearl Harbor attack—an irony that amused the late actor.[49]

From the Japanese perspective, the Yashimas' story is bittersweet, even sorrowful. *Good-Bye Japan: The Exile of Picture Book Artists Taro and Mitsuko Yashima* is the title of Usami Shō's 1981 Japanese-language biography of the couple. Although the biography is about both husband and wife, the title is a better reflection of Taro's attitude. The past misinterpretation of his wartime activities seems to have haunted the artist. "No one says I'm against my country now," the seventy-four-year-old Yashima asserted in 1982, as if to reassure himself.[50] By then, he had resided in the United States for over forty years, but "my country" still referred to Japan, a nation of which he remained a citizen. Even after a stroke in 1977, he held on to an ambition to go back to Japan and open an art studio, but was never able to do so, his son explained.

In 1942, when Jun and Tomoe decided to use pseudonyms, they chose the surname Yashima, using the Chinese characters that meant "eight islands." It was not an idle choice, as they used Chinese characters not commonly used for this name. Theirs was an allusion to Ōyashima, the "great eight provinces" or islands produced by the union of the gods Izanami and Izanagi in Japan's creation myth. Taro referred to Kintarō, the hero of a Japanese folk tale.[51] Although his OSS supervisors touted his "loyalty" to the United States, he identified strongly as a Japanese. It was through love of Japan that he urged Japanese soldiers to cease fighting and live to see their families back home. But distinguishing love for the country and "the people" from loyalty to state was, and remains, difficult to do, especially during wartime, as antiwar activists know all too well. As Yashima once did, many Americans are wondering today about the meaning of patriotism—whether one can be loyal to fellow Americans yet refuse to support the U.S. state in a time of war. Yashima's transnational odyssey, though inspiring, is perhaps sobering; it reminds us that however much non-state actors try to work across national boundaries, they often cannot escape demands for fidelity to the state.

Notes

I thank Monisha DasGupta, Cindy Franklin, Erika Lee, Andy Lohmeier, Greg Robinson, Gordon Chang, and Kerry Smith for their help and valuable suggestions.

1. Advertisement by Henry Holt & Company, 257 Fourth Ave, New York, for *The New Sun* by Taro Yashima, *Saturday Review of Literature,* January 27, 1945, 6.

2. Christopher Lazare, "Japanese Liberal," *New York Times Book Review,* November 21, 1943, 6. Lazare wrote that *The New Sun* "makes reassuring reading for those of us who still like to believe that independence is an inevitable human instinct that even the most vicious systems cannot entirely outlaw or obliterate."

3. All quotes in this paragraph from the Henry Holt advertisement, except those attributed to the *New York Times.*

4. The pen-and-ink sketch of Carlos Bulosan by Francis O'Brien Garfield, who drew most of the *Saturday Review*'s cover art during this period, is the cover image on the edition of *America Is in the Heart* that is currently being published by the University of Washington Press.

5. See Richard H. Minear, *Dr. Seuss Goes to War: The World War II Editorial Cartoons of Theodor Seuss Geisel* (New York: New Press, 1999).

6. This line came from Frank Capra's documentary *"Know Your Enemy—Japan"* from the U.S. Army's *Why We Fight* series. John W. Dower points out that it was a fairly common image, used by other Americans during the war. Dower, *War Without Mercy: Race & Power in the Pacific War* (New York: Pantheon, 1987), 366, note 9.

7. It is difficult to ascertain how well *The New Sun* was known in the United States, although we know that it never appeared on a best seller list and, until now, was never reprinted in this country. See note 22 below. Much later, in 1991, Yashima's sequel to *The New Sun, Horizon Is Calling* (1947), was excerpted in a collection of Asian American writing. Jeffrey Paul Chan, Frank Chin, Lawson Fusao Inada, and Shawn Wong, *The Big Aiiieeeee! An Anthology of Chinese American and Japanese American Literature* (New York: Plume, 1991), 246–303.

8. In Yashima's text, *tokkōka* appears as Tokkoka, omitting the macron to symbolize that the second *o* is a long vowel. The *tokkōka* was a division of the secret police, the *tokkō* or *tokukō.* Both these two words, derived respectively from *tokkōkeisatsu* and *tokubetsukōkeisatsu*, literally mean "special high police." Until it was disbanded after World War II by U.S. Occupation authorities, the *tokkō* was charged with suppressing dissent and "antiestablishment" activities.

9. Later recalled by his wife. See Mitsu Yashima, "My Father and Me," *New Dawn*, November 1974, 8–11. Though foregrounded as a story about her relationship

with her father, this article tells Mitsu's version of the same experience. I thank Greg Robinson for giving me a copy of this article.

10. Yashima calls it a "confession," in quotation marks to imply that it was a false statement. More accurately, as mentioned above it was probably a *tenkō* statement—a statement of repudiation, not a confession. Yashima, *The New Sun*, 296.

11. Mitsu later explained that the advanced state of her pregnancy caused her to capitulate and submit a *tenkō*. As her baby grew inside her abdomen, he put enormous pressure on her bladder, but as her husband described in *The New Sun*, the *tokkōka* permitted the prisoners to go to the toilet only twice a day. No special dispensation was given to Mitsu as a pregnant woman. The humiliation of having to relieve herself in the cell was made worse by shame of causing her cellmates—who had so considerately given her the most food and the most comfortable spot in the cell—to have to suffer from the stench. But decades later, Mitsu continued to express regret and feelings of shame for having to repudiate her principles and, in so doing, betray her comrades. See Mitsu Yashima, "My Father and Me."

12. Not much exists in English on Yashima's life besides his two graphic autobiographies, *The New Sun* (New York: Henry Holt & Co., 1943) and *Horizon Is Calling* (New York: Henry Holt & Co., 1947). The Taro Yashima Papers, mostly pertaining to his children's books, are housed in the de Grummond Collection at the University of Southern Mississippi. This Web site provides a brief biography: http://www.lib.usm.edu/%7Edegrum/html/research/findaids/yashima.htm. There is also a Web site by a former art student: http://taroyashima.homestead.com/Page1.html. The most extensive works on Yashima's life are in Japanese: a documentary, a book-length biography, and several articles—see the bibliography of Shō Usami, *Sayonara Nippon: Ehon sakka, Yashima Tarō to Mitsuko no bōmei* (Tokyo: Shōbunsha, 1981), 320–321. Another biography of Yashima in Japanese is being written by his former student, Masakiyo Watanabe. Watanabe, a writer and retired civil engineer living in the Los Angeles area, knew Yashima for over thirty years. An English-language study of Mitsu Yashima is being completed by UCLA history professor Valerie J. Matsumoto.

13. The Chinese character used for Jun can also be read as "Atsushi," and Iwamatsu also went by this pronunciation.

14. Momo Yashima Brannen, telephone interview, March 8, 2005.

15. Joseph C. Green, chief, Special Division, Department of State, telegram sent to Taka Ayabe and forty-nine other Japanese aliens residing in New York City, June 1, 1942, DOS files, National Archives, Washington, D.C.

16. Mitsu Yashima, "Letter to Mako to Meet Again," *Common Ground* (November 1949), 41–46; quote on p. 42. Mitsu's pain, sorrow, and regret about leaving their son behind in Japan are quite palpable here.

17. Usami, *Sayonara Nippon*, 189–190.

18. Mitsu recalled her husband being unable to sleep at night, tormented by the fear that great harm would come to Mako as the son of a "traitor." This was especially true after he finished but had not yet published *The New Sun*. At this point, it was Mitsu who showed fortitude and tried to convince Taro that her family would do their utmost to keep Mako safe. "Letter to Mako," 42; "My Father and Me," 11.

19. From Yashima's preface to the 1978 Japanese-language edition of *The New Sun*. Yashima Tarō, *Atarashii taiyō* (Tokyo: Shōbunsha, 1978), 10.

20. Yashima, however, had another son through a relationship he had with another woman before marrying his wife, and this son never immigrated to the United States. See note 44.

21. Yashima, *Atarashii taiyō*, 9.

22. The *Saturday Review*'s assessment of *America Is in the Heart* was that it was "a book which should make Americans ashamed of themselves" and thus essential reading for intelligent Americans of good will. "People interested in driving from America the scourge of intolerance should read Mr. Bulosan's autobiography. They should read it that they may draw from the anger it will arouse in them the determination to bring to an end the vicious nonsense of racism." Although Bulosan "makes no effort to spare the reader's nerves," he understood that "given a chance, the average person would prefer to be decent." The reviewer noted approvingly that Bulosan was neither strident nor shrill, and did not resort to accusatory name-calling. In other words, Bulosan's narrative allowed much more privileged American readers to be critical of themselves but not overly so. William S. Lynch, "Loyalty in Spite of All," *Saturday Review of Literature*, March 9, 1946, 7–8.

23. Exact numbers of the sale of *The New Sun* could not be determined. In 1998, Henry Holt's senior publicist told me that the records of *The New Sun*'s sales might be buried in some box somewhere in the company building(s), but that it would be difficult and time-consuming for them to retrieve the information. In other words, the company had no archivist or user-friendly archive. Henry Holt, by this time, had been purchased by the German publishing conglomerate, Verlagsgruppe Georg von Holtzbrinck GmbH. The senior publicist, however, gave me Taro Yashima's actual name. I wrote to Jun Iwamatsu, and received a letter from his son, Makoto, telling me that his father had passed away. The son did not know whether the book sold well, but he guessed it did well enough for Henry Holt to publish its sequel, *Horizon Is Calling* (1947). Elizabeth Shreve, Senior Publicist, Henry Holt & Company, phone conversation, January 9, 1998; Makoto Iwamatsu, letter, February 18, 1998.

24. On national character studies, see Dower, *War Without Mercy*, ch. 6; for psywar, see Allison B. Gilmore, *You Can't Fight Tanks with Bayonets: Psychological*

Warfare against the Japanese Army in the Southwest Pacific (Lincoln: University of Nebraska Press, 1998).

25. See Naoko Shibusawa, *America's Geisha Ally: Re-Imagining the Japanese Enemy* (Cambridge, Mass.: Harvard University Press, 2006).

26. Tobias Moss to Hon. Tom C. Clark, Attorney General, May 11, 1946, exhibit 6, congressional file re: S. 1409/H. 2379 Public Law 400.

27. Yashima Tarō, *Atarashiki Taiyō: Nihonbun setsumeiban* (S.I.: s.n., 1943); idem, *Atarashiki Taiyō* (Tokyo: Chuōsha, 1949).

28. CIA personnel file, RG 263, National Archives, College Park. The OSS personnel files list the couple by their actual names, Iwamatsu, not their pseudonym of Yashima.

29. Mitsu broadcasted, she later stated to journalist Judy Stone, to Japanese women to urge them to give up the war effort. Judy Stone, "An Unlikely Heroine of World War II," *San Francisco Chronicle*, March 18, 2007, <http://www.sfgate.com/cgi-bin/article.cgi?f=/c/a/2007/03/18/PKGSLOJSV11.DTL&feed=rss.entertainment> accessed May 18, 2007.

30. Iwatsubo, Personal History Statement; memorandum, Lester Y. Baylis, security officer, to personnel officer, OSS (M[orale]O[perations]-F[ar]E[ast]), August 19, 1944. Both documents in Iwatsubo file, OSS personnel files, RG 226, National Archives, College Park.

31. Telephone interview with Masakiyo Watanabe, January 17, 2006.

32. Watanabe recalls his father having this reaction to Yashima after meeting him during a trip to Los Angeles from Japan around 1973. Ibid. It is possible that Yashima's story continues to provoke an impression that he was a traitor. Indeed, this is how my mother, a Japanese expatriate living in the United States, first reacted when I told her the story a few years ago.

33. For an example of Issei references to the United States as "the enemy," see Hawai'i journalist Sōga Yasutarō's memoir of his internment at Sand Island and in a Department of Justice camp in Santa Fe. Originally published in Japanese in 1948 with the title, *Tessaku no seikatsu*, Soga's memoirs have recently been published in an English translation with an introduction by Tetsuden Kashima of the University of Washington. Yasutaro Soga, *Life Behind Barbed Wire: The World War II Interment Memoirs of a Hawaii Issei*, trans. Kihei Hirai (Honolulu: University of Hawai'i Press, 2008).

34. "For Services Rendered," *New York Times*, June 1, 1946, 11.

35. For an English-language description of that Japanese expatriate community in New York by one of its members, see the memoir of feminist Ayako Ishigaki. Ayako Ishigaki, *Restless Wave: My Life in Two Worlds, A Memoir* with an afterword by Yi-Chun Tricia Lin and Greg Robinson (1940; reprint, New York: Feminist Press at City University of New York, 2004). See also Greg Robinson, "Nisei in Gotham:

The JACD and Japanese Americans in 1940s New York," *Prospects: An Annual of American Cultures Studies* 30 (2005): 581–595.

36. Senator [Pat] McCarran to Senator [Chapman] Revercomb, memorandum re: S. 1409, Docket 596, n.d.; William H. E. Acker to the chairmen of the Senate and House Judiciary Committee, n.d., exhibit 5; Robert A. Saltzstein, Memorandum in Support of Senate bill 1409, House Bill 2379, n.d., exhibit 4; Herbert S. Little to Senator Warren G. Magnuson, March 27, 1948, exhibit 3. All documents in congressional file re: S. 1409/H. 2379 Private Law 400, National Archives, Washington, D.C.

37. Because the preoccupation was on image, rather than on the difficult task of thoroughly overhauling institutionalized racism, this federal support to end racial discrimination did little to eliminate a system of racial hierarchy and privilege in the United States. Mary L. Dudziak, *Cold War Civil Rights: Race and the Image of American Democracy* (Princeton: Princeton University Press, 2000); Thomas Borstelmann, *Cold War and the Color Line: Race Relations in the Global Arena* (Cambridge, Mass.: Harvard University Press, 2001); Yukiko Koshiro, *Transpacific Racisms and the U.S. Occupation of Japan* (New York: Columbia University Press, 1999).

38. Senator McCarran to Senator Revercomb, memorandum re: S. 1409, Docket 596, n.d., congressional file re: S. 1409/H. 2379. Revercomb penciled "OK" and initialed this memo.

39. See Koshiro, *Transpacific Racisms*.

40. "For the relief of Markoto [*sic*] Iwamatsu," 80th Congress, Senate Bill 1409, June 10, 1947; Private Law 400, passed June 29, 1948, *80th Congress Statutes at Large*, vol. 62, p. 1395; *80th Congress, 2nd session, Senate Reports*, vol. 1324, Report No. 1324; *80th Congress, 2nd session, House Reports*, vol. 11212, Report No. 2275.

41. Pat Clark, "Japanese Boyhood" [review of *The Village Tree*], *New York Times Book Review*, November 15, 1953, 43.

42. Quoted in http://www.lib.usm.edu/~degrum/html/research/findaids/yashima.htm#bio; see also Taro Yashima, "On Making a Book for a Child," *Horn Book*, February 1955, 21–24.

43. A Web search for *The Crow Boy* shows that it continues to be used in "Multicultural Lesson Plans" and in teachers' resources to promote acceptance of differences among children. See, for example, http://jeffcoweb.jeffco.k12.co.us/passport/lessonplan/lessons/belong.html.

44. Much earlier in their marriage, Mitsu had to contend with another woman, although this woman was in Taro's past. One day, when she was pregnant with Mako, a strange woman appeared at their home. She asked to see Taro, saying that his son wanted to meet his father. Momo recalls her mother telling her this, but she was not aware of a half-brother until she was in her teens. The Japanese-language sources say that this woman and Taro had a relationship that was broken off when the woman's

father ordered her to stop seeing a poor artist with suspicious leftist politics. This son grew up without his father and became a well-known author. Momo Yashima, January 12, 2007; Usami; Sodei Rinjirō "*Bei senryaku jōhōkyoku* (OSS) *ni kyōryoku shita nihonjin gaka*" [The Japanese Artist Who Collaborated with the U.S. Strategic Military Intelligence Bureau (OSS)], *Playboy* (Japanese edition), August 1979, 102, 113. I am grateful to Eiichiro Azuma for sending me a copy of this article.

45. Momo Yashima, telephone interview, January 12, 2006. For more on Mitsu Yashima, see Valerie J. Matsumoto's forthcoming piece on this activist-artist.

46. Yashima, *Atarashii taiyō*, 9

47. Sodei, *Bei senryaku jōhōkyoku*, 101–113. Quote on pp. 101, 102.

48. Departing slightly from Benedict Anderson's famous definition of nationalism as "imagined communities," I am using Robert H. Wiebe's definition because his emphasizes the emotive appeal of nationalism more strongly and with more empathy. Also, the distinction I make about Yashima's nationalism differs slightly from the one Mae Ngai makes regarding the political support and cultural affinity for Japan among Japanese Americans. I am suggesting a strongly felt bond with the people and the place more so than affinity with the people with a common cultural tradition. Robert H. Wiebe, *Who We Are: A History of Popular Nationalism* (Princeton: Princeton University Press, 2002), ch. 1; Mae M. Ngai, *Impossible Subjects: Illegal Aliens and the Making of Modern America* (Princeton: Princeton University Press, 2004), ch. 5, esp. p. 180.

49. Makoto Iwamatsu, telephone interview, April 18, 2005. Acting runs in the family. His sister, Momo, and his two daughters, Mimosa and Sala, are also established actors, as was his mother, Mitsu. This extraordinary woman appeared in the television movie, *Farewell to Manzanar* (1976), with both Mako and Momo, as well as in movies such as *Foul Play* (1978) and *Oh God, Book II* (1980).

50. David Holley, "Japanese Artist Who Aided U.S. in War Finds Acceptance," *Los Angeles Times,* August 2, 1982.

51. Ibid.; Sodei, *Bei senryaku jōhōkyoku*, 108. I could not find a reference to Mitsu, but Mitsuko literally means "child of sunrays."

Part 1

THE SUNNY HOUSE

It was in 1933, at the end of spring, that my wife and I moved
to the eastern part of Tokyo.

The house had a small yard, unusual in this district of poor people, where our baby could play.

When we walked in the open field beyond the yard, we could
see the little houses of the city's factory workers.

The house was sunny, and we were outdoors most of the time.
The baby's cheeks soon turned brown.

I fertilized the poor soil and we planted our first flower and
vegetable garden.

Best of all, there was a neighborhood nursery where we could leave the baby while we worked to earn more money.

We began to celebrate by giving the baby an extra bottle of milk every day.

Now we could enjoy the traditional custom of exchanging gifts
with our new neighbors.

Workers came from their homes to pose for my wife and me.

We set up large new canvases, planning pictures that would have a deeper reality than any before.

Part 2

A BUNCH OF DAFFODILS

One morning, a month later, the nursery was closed without warning by the Tokkoka, the Japanese secret police.

With no nursery, all the babies had to be cared for at home,
or by neighbors.

One morning after our own baby had been at a neighbor's house he seemed strangely listless.

Early the next day he was dead.

Soft smoke rose into the May sky.

A friend and I painted my wife, whose breast was so lonely
now.

One of our models brought a poem in which he mourned his
little friend.

A few mornings later my wife said, "I won't cry any more."
She had a new baby inside her.

That evening I brought home a bunch of daffodils from the city. As I stood outside, I thought it strange that the house was so bright and yet so quiet.

Inside the house there was no wife, no usual atmosphere of supper. Three men were waiting for me.

As we left the house, one man hooked each arm; the third followed. I knew they were taking me to the Tokkoka office, but they slapped me when I asked why.

The prison, which already held my wife, was in darkness except for the lighted section which housed the Tokkoka.

Part 3

THE CAVE

In the morning at a few minutes before five o'clock the jail guard roared: "Hey, get up! Get out of there!" The men in my cell scrambled to their feet.

Washing time was thirty seconds. The prisoners splashed their faces hurriedly, looking as if they were stealing the water.

Investigations always began at nine o'clock, but one day followed another and still neither my wife nor I was called.

We felt our spirits grow feeble, just sitting all day. If one of us talked, he was taken out into the corridor to sit alone.

Anyone caught asleep was jabbed with a bamboo stick.

The only occupation we were allowed was the study of the
habits of the louse and the best methods of capturing it.

Toilet times were three a day. Growing accustomed to this
was as difficult as if we were all first-graders again.

In the late afternoon the harsh sounds of the officers' ken-jutsu and jujutsu exercises broke the sleepy silence.

In the evening those who had been called up for investigation came back. . . . Some of the political prisoners, unrecognizable in their misery, could hardly reach their cells.

Often they were brought back unconscious.

On the neck of a Korean boy who was dumped into our cell
one evening were five cigarette burns.

On the covers of the food boxes we were given was an elegant label, but the contents smelled revolting.

Actually, the food was culled from garbage thrown out of restaurants.

One day, when my cellmates had stomach poisoning, I thought enviously of donkeys who get their nourishment from straw.

No matter how bad the food was, if a short-term prisoner
had any money he had to pay ten sen for each meal.

The covers of the lunch boxes were scratched. The scratches
said: "Actual price 2 sen, head of police station 4 sen, boss of
restaurant 4 sen. YOU are the thieves!"

During the nights we were fairly comfortable if we could all lie down, even in tight rows like sardines, but usually a few people had to stand.

If there were more than twenty of us, we were like potatoes in a sack.

Men and women flowed into the prison as if through Tokyo's
sewers — every night, never stopping.

I was awakened many times by the same passion — a terrible
desire to hold our baby on my knee.

But . . . the baby was dead.

My wife and I had only occasional glimpses of each other to
help us keep our courage.

Part 4

GUARDS AND PRISONERS

The guards outside the iron bars were surprising creatures.

One, in particular, never grew tired of baiting us. He could
easily spend a whole day threatening and intimidating the
prisoners.

He enjoyed looking into the women's cell at midnight and seemed to regard this as one of the special advantages of his job.

At other times he tweaked hairs from his nose, polished his shoes, or ate cakes bought with the prisoners' lunch payments.

Another guard was a poet. One day I saw him working hard
to combine flowering plants and the grades on his daughter's
report card into one poem.

But this poet's humanity was a doubtful thing. If we asked for something, he would raise his eyes toward the ceiling and say, "I am not a high officer."

Very often I had a feeling that these creatures were strange,
nameless animals. Compared to them all the prisoners were
truly human.

One of the prisoners was a newsboy who had done nothing more than look into a factory through a hole in the wall.

An old man's offense was that the forty yen in his pocket had
not seemed in keeping with his poor clothes.

A Korean garbage man was in prison for trying to steal one zinc pipe. As he said, this was nothing compared to Japan's seizure of all Korea.

The drunken prisoners used to taunt the guard: "Ha, ha, a
low salary and a tin sword! Everybody's laughing up his
sleeve at you!"

The harder they were beaten the more grandiose were the words they used. "Oh, despotism! This is despotism!"

The political prisoners' feeling of superiority was unbearable to the guards. One Korean boy was always smiling, though he was only a ragamuffin.

A member of the labor union of an iron factory maintained
a serene aloofness unsuitable to a worker.

With one blow the guard struck down an underground
worker who gave a false name.

When the beautiful daughter of a famous economist was
brought in, the guard observed slyly, "Well, this is the age
when even professors' daughters go to jail."

One day an unexpected prisoner was brought in — it was
Doctor Yama.

Doctor Yama was well known in this district because his office was open to the poor people.

He had gone to the Tokkoka with his lawyer in an attempt
to have my pregnant wife set free, and had been sentenced to
jail for it.

Not only was my wife forbidden better food, but when she
obstinately demanded it the guard slapped her in the face
with a slipper.

Guarding against the rough, crowded people, eating the remains of her cellmates' food greedily, the mother fought desperately to preserve her baby's life.

Finally she was called for questioning by the Tokkoka. I said
to myself, "If it will help to set her free, I will stay here for
another month, two months, half a year."

Suddenly I heard her voice from somewhere upstairs, screaming, screaming.

The sound set me afire. New baby, unborn baby, your father can do nothing for you now. Please don't stop living!

Part 5

TOKKOKA

Three months passed without our being investigated or
questioned. The light that came through the small prison
windows told us that summer was at hand.

Through my cellmates who were being investigated, the character of the Tokkoka was becoming clearer to me.

I heard that my wife's mother had come to the Tokkoka from the city of Sendai. She had made the chief furious by using the word "humanity" in telling him that her daughter was pregnant.

My sister, too, had come to the jail, but had been sent away
without seeing us.

Some of my friends, painters, had tried to testify for us, but the chief had snarled at them, "Are you requesting or ordering? Which?"

My brother, I was told, had sent a registered letter to the Tokkoka. Perhaps he had enclosed a money order for me, but we never saw it.

When a workman friend came to see us, the Tokkoka telephoned to headquarters to make sure that he was not a
wanted man before they would let him go.

I also heard that our landlord had been told we were worse than a pair of thieves. He had found our house ransacked after the police's search, and reported that it had been robbed.

Of course the Tokkoka refused to let our visitors see us, but
they gladly took the cakes and fruits that were brought for
us. All the same, I was sustained by the knowledge of our
friends' loyalty.

And then, at last, we were called for investigation. It was
already the middle of summer.

As soon as I stepped into the office of the Tokkoka, the chief roared: "Well, have you given in? You might as well; I never allow even one dangerous prisoner to go free in my district!"

"Baby? After you've had a good time, don't blubber!" The chief laughed at my wife's pleading.

Finally he gave his orders: "I permit you both to write your
personal histories, starting tomorrow. Nothing can be done
before that. Go back to your cells!"

"Personal histories" — obviously they were to show the Tokkoka everything that was inside us, like an X-ray.

Part 6
PERSONAL HISTORY: FIRST AMBITION

Tosa, a province in the southern part of the main Japanese island, was famous because the power that broke the feudal system in Japan had its beginnings there.

About eighty years ago a certain low-class samurai wandered
onto a peninsula of this region.

The samurai chose a plot of earth and built a little house
with the help of the village people.

Thirty years after the Meiji Revolution, his son built a new house which had painted on it a red cross, the symbol of the doctor's profession he had chosen. This was my parents' home.

The first thing that I can remember is our family group eating, presided over by my mother.

My father was always reading difficult books on medicine, sitting in the same formal position.

The story of the Meiji Revolution, the story of the French
Revolution, tales of Chinese and Japanese national heroes —
my father's talks, often held in the bathtub, were my first
schooling.

Father's bookcase was an interesting storehouse. There I met
the rabbits of Toba Sojo and the humorous Yedo citizens of
Hokusai.

I liked to make pictures for myself, too; every wall was a
place to paint.

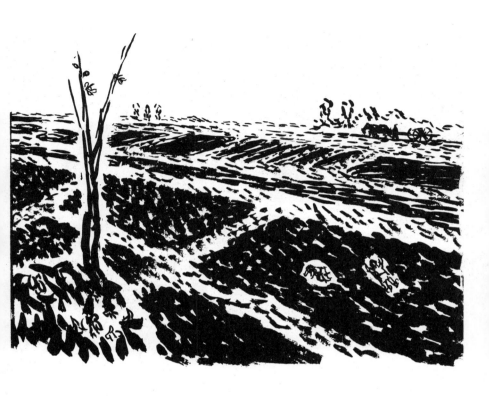

In the spring our neighborhood was covered with flowers and young leaves and filled with their fragrance.

On the river bank, in the summer, we played in the big trees
which stretched toward the burning sun.

In the autumn fields the golden waves of rice reflected the
high blue sky.

In the winter, the gold of tangerines wove the farmers'
houses together in a bright pattern.

All my friends were farmers' children. They were geniuses
who could make straw sandals and birdhouses.

The father that I remember best was always with the sick
and injured people of the village.

When the big power dam near our village was built, he
worked like many-armed Kwannon to save the farmers who
were badly hurt in the dangerous work.

"The peoples of the world are brothers. Doctors are made for humanity." Father often said those words, and he treated people in need wherever he met them.

Finally the day came when I was to go to the high school in
a nearby city. Although I liked to paint, I also had dreams of
becoming an admiral.

Part 7

TO BE A PAINTER

At the high school in the city which had a population of
eighteen thousand people, I had to get used to unexpected
new ways.

The teachers' ideas did not inspire me. Studying soon became a cold, formal duty.

Army officers taught us physical drill. They were very different from what I had imagined military men would be like.

My dream of becoming an admiral began to fade. Then came news of my mother's death. . . .

When I went back to my village many questions rose up
within me. . . . Why were the faces of my old friends so
gloomy?

What did the farmers mean when they muttered: "Students don't know the price of rice!"

Back in the city again, I sometimes felt that the classroom was in the depths of the ocean and that the teacher was an octopus wearing glasses.

Reading the books sent by my older brother, who was studying at the university in Tokyo, was better than listening to
teachers.

And then, one day a painting by an impressionist opened my
eyes to the strong, rich color and light of the world.

But "soft boys" like me who thought about other things than physical education were especially hated by our jujutsu and kenjutsu teachers.

An army officer, our instructor in military drill, once hit me in the face with a book which I had been carrying in my pocket.

This kind of brutality only strengthened my determination to become a painter.

School became nothing but a place from which I could get my graduation certificate. Sketching outdoors took most of my time.

During the vacation when I saw my father for the last time, he assented to my ambition. "That's all right. It is as difficult to be a real artist as it is to be an admiral."

Part 8

WHERE ARE WE GOING?

Tokyo next — the capital and center of modern Japan, where
I went at the end of my high-school career.

I was one of the students appointed by the government to the Japanese Imperial Art Academy.

But when I encountered the terrible disorder of modern art,
my mind was thrown into complete confusion.

On the one hand, the realism of the Imperial professors had
no inner spirit, and on the other, the moderns who went
further than realism seemed to have only a destructive purpose.

Where in all this land was there a steady foundation for my
mind and body? Where would I find real creation?

My beloved older brother was a poet. He also was filled with
loneliness and confusion, and could guide me no longer.

There was only one thing to do — draw close to the friends
who were looking for the same things I was. . . . Three of us
rented a small house.

Where did we come from? Where are we now?

What is love? That is finding a wife, we said. But what is
life?

What is fighting? That is the defeat of evil. . . . But what is good?

And then, where are we going?

One night I fell down drunk in the washroom of a restaurant
on the outskirts of Tokyo and couldn't get up from the floor
until daylight.

Somehow I had lost my way in the city. One day I determined
to go back to the village that was my home.

There I found farmers' babies dying because no one could
afford a doctor. My father had taken care of them, but now
he was dead.

Poor people who were in debt lost what they had left. My father's records of unpaid bills were sold to people in the village who made the farmers pay more than they owed.

The poorest farmers' families, who had lost even their fields,
were leaving for other places.

I began a search for light. Once, I decorated my portrait of a little working girl with wild spring flowers.

But thought seemed helpless in contrast to the human history
that had been silently piling up . . . the countless graves of
farmers.

One day some Beethoven records left by my brother hit me
like thunder. . . . "Get up! Find! Catch the power of your
new generation!"

Quickly I went back to my friends and the Academy at Tokyo
and began to read wildly — books on economic history, social
history, the history of philosophy, the history of art, social
psychology, the philosophy of laughter.

Books that told how humans were in the past, how humans are now, how humans will be in the future.

Finally I was expelled from the Academy for being absent
from military drill. And for having struck the superintendent
when he wouldn't listen to my explanation.

I was no longer a student who would become a high-school art teacher and live in an up-to-date residence at the state's expense. Instead, I was only one of the newest and least successful illustrators for cheap magazines.

One evening, after a day in which I hadn't earned a single
penny, I heard some railroad workers singing their song. It
vibrated with strength and brightness.

Part 9

THE ARTIST BELONGS TO THE PEOPLE

Theories of art which seemed to have the freshness of a new
age set me off in another new direction.

Yes, in any period the real artist belongs to the people who are creating history.

We must wash off this corrupt, modern lifelessness. We must go ahead to establish a healthy realism.

My friends and I joined an art movement which had a progressive philosophy.

Our purpose was to understand people's reality. There, metal
was hidden which artists had never mined before.

In one dimension, anyway, my life became settled upon. I married a girl who was trying as hard as I was to find reality in art.

Every morning I used to mix with the crowd at a government employment office to learn about people who had no work or money.

My wife, for her part, lived in a farmer's home near Tokyo
in order to understand how farmers live.

We felt that we had to find a power rising up in the people which could stop the militarism, the oppression, the fascism of our time. We, and other artists, got in touch with the underground movement, and learned how the people were being organized.

Soon a people's art exhibition was opened. Nothing of its
kind had ever before been held. Attendance was very large,
compared to other exhibitions.

Smaller exhibitions traveled from crowded factory zones to farmers' villages.

Reproductions and picture magazines were published so that
we could get to the people in their homes.

I made many pictures of different kinds. Once, after a whole
village had refused to drill for the army, I tried to express
a scornful laugh at the militarists.

Another time I tried to demonstrate that the construction work which we were told was for unemployment relief was actually exploiting the workers and preparing for war.

One of my pictures showed that the courtroom at the sup-
posedly public trial of political prisoners was being filled
with thugs gathered by the police.

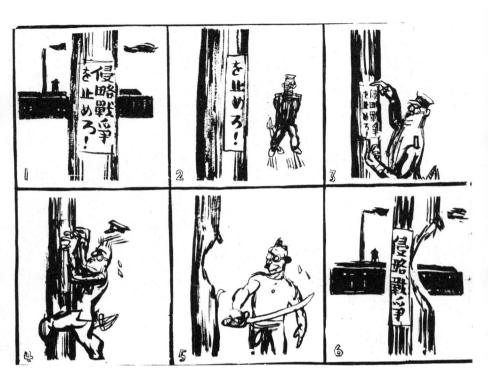

"Stop the war of aggression in China!" The words were
posted everyhere. We made the government's attitude
toward the progressive movement the subject of many comic
strips.

In every field — law, medicine, music, motion pictures, literature, drama — the movement was active.

In many districts "culture clubs" were organized in which all groups of the movement took part.

On the roof of the studio of the artists' association was painted, "Come! Study! New, progressive art studio."

"Will a new Japan be born?"

"Look, we are building it every moment! Soon the day will come when the people will stand up for it."

Part 10

THE FLAG IN THE STORM

The storm which broke over Manchuria, destroying the freedom of the Manchurian and Chinese people, also began to blow through the islands of Japan.

At exhibitions the police ordered us to cover parts of paintings and change their names. Many paintings were taken
away entirely.

At artists' meetings there was always a crowd of policemen, ready for trouble. Speakers were arrested for using a word like "oppression."

Publications were censored more harshly all the time, so that words, passages, and whole pages were crossed out. Some issues were seized and not allowed to be sold.

Artists accompanying traveling exhibitions found, in one
place after another, that the exhibitions were prohibited.
Sometimes they themselves disappeared; we found out later
that they had been arrested.

Life became very hard for all of us. Newspapers and magazines refused to use our work, and those of us who had regular jobs began to lose them.

Electricity, gas, and water were shut off because we could not pay for them. The police and their thugs became interested in the question of our rent.

Underground movements, driven down deeper, used the culture groups as the only way to rebuild their memberships. The character of the organizers who came to us became worse as the more experienced leaders were arrested.

Although our group was faced with difficult and complicated problems, some of our new, unskillful leaders lashed at us with biting, "revolutionary" words.

It was the same with our work — their criticism was nothing more than a slap in the face. The passion for creative work faded.

There was no way to go ahead — only one picture magazine was being published, and that secretly, like an underground paper.

The pictures in the magazine became dark and poor, and they always had the same title: "Fight back against the storm of terrorism!"

Though the slogan was "Double the number of readers," the magazine was actually losing many of the readers it had.

To get money to carry on, we had no choice but to take it
from our friends, at every chance, in the name of progress.

The number of men who could not be considered real artists, political organizers, or union leaders increased. The studio which was once flourishing now became a lodging for mock intellectuals.

The baby — our first — who was born in our house was wel-
comed by the eyes of worried people, and choked with the
nervous cigarette smoke of the celebration.

It was obvious to my wife and me that there could be no theory or work or magazine away from the daily life of the people. We determined to live among the workers, so we had moved into the eastern part of the city.

But the storm had swept over our new home. Our baby had died. The new baby, who was now coming, might not live.

I could not imagine how the flag of culture that had been flown with honor until recently could be carried forward.

"But the great need of the people for this culture is an historic fact. There is no one who can stifle it." With these words I ended my personal history.

Part II

THE NEW REALITY

Less than a week after I finished my personal history, I was
made to sit down in an empty room.

Members of the Tokkoka surrounded me, with the tools of
their profession. Of course I had expected that violent punishment would come some time. This was it.

Chairs, shoes, wooden swords, and rubber hoses fell on me
until I lost consciousness.

A few days later, the Tokkoka ordered the guard to cut my hair short.

Out of the jail, suddenly — but only to go to the army's annual roll-call as a new recruit for the reserves of my district.

In an atmosphere full of menace the inspector, a lieutenant
colonel, barked that "The present official will review you in
the name of His Imperial Majesty!"

A soldier whose pronunciation was poor because of bad teeth was knocked on the jaw. "Why don't you get false teeth? Are you afraid of the dentist?"

A man who wore a badge on his shirt was handed over to the military police. "Search out the group this bum belongs to."

There were bruises on my face from the day spent with the Tokkoka. "Stupid, you must be a thug if you like to fight so much!"

After the roll-call, when we came back from lunch, many
guns were stacked in waiting for us.

All of us were ordered to charge from one end of the field
to the other, one hundred, two hundred times. Several men
fainted.

When the surviving recruits were lined up in a row, the
inspector came along to show us how bad we were. "Do you
think you can kill a man with your kind of charging?"

After he had ordered us to break ranks and then to fall in, twenty or thirty times, he snarled, "I've got to get you closer under my arm!"

Lecture and lesson followed the drilling. First many Imperial
sayings were read.

Lecture — After you throw out Western thought and its students, who corrupt the Japanese nation, you yourselves must be masters in the East.

Lesson — How many times larger than Japan is Manchukuo?
Why does Lenin's staue in Leningrad stand point-
ing at Japan?
Why do we have to fight America and England?

If we answered, "I don't know," the inspector said, "Say
what you think." If we answered, "I forget," he pressed us:
"So. Did you know before?"

If we wanted to sit down without answering, he mocked us:
"Hey, the enemy's tanks are coming at you. You can't stand
silent!"

At last, in the evening, discharged men went home silently.
I was put back in my cell again.

In September and October, air raid drills became frequent. The whole jail was covered with a black cloth throughout the night.

On the nights of air raid drills the sweat falling from my
neck onto my neighbor's leg flowed together with his sweat
and rolled down between us.

By midnight I could hear my wife moaning. But the black cloth prevented me from seeing even the window of her cell.

Part 12

BAD DREAM

The sunlight coming in through the window grew weaker
day by day. Winter was coming.

Also, a "confession" written by a famous underground leader,
who had thereby been released, made us feel colder.

False confessions were forced from underground leaders by the Tokkoka. Each new prisoner had to read them before writing his own personal history.

It became clear that political prisoners who "confessed" were well treated by the Tokkoka.

In the middle of a restless night I saw one of these betrayers
called by the Tokkoka. He went out very cheerfully, as if it
had all been arranged beforehand.

Prisoners of this kind soon went free, anyway — never even saying good-by to companions who had been sharing their suffering.

We suspected that it was their duty to help in arresting their
friends, that this was the condition on which they had been
given freedom so soon.

Prisoners who were unconvinced by the "confessions" were punished both brutally and subtly. One of my cellmates was made to hold all his confiscated books in the air every afternoon.

Others were sentenced to five, ten, or fifteen years, or life, in prison . . . as it suited the Tokkoka.

Every night, now, nearly everybody, the union organizer, the
political organizer, the Korean boy, the culture group worker,
and others, had miserable nightmares.

Even worse, the nightmares that attacked these prisoners made them physically sick, one by one.

The police doctor came rarely. His first duty was to find out
whether anyone was going to die.

According to the medical science of this doctor, itch was a
helpless illness, boils broke by themselves, the nerves of decayed teeth died by themselves, and gastric ulcers were a
matter of fate.

Not until December did this doctor allow my wife to leave
the prison. Nine months with child, she carried out her body
inch by inch, unable to bend or stretch.

Her smiling eyes had told me that she would surely bear our
baby. I was afraid that the baby might not be born alive . . .
but its mother *must* live.

Now a cold, dreary winter rain was falling in every political prisoner's mind. All the work we had done seemed to melt away in futility.

Part 13

JAIL NEWS

The new year came. It reminded us that our only home now
was the jail. But our cell came also to seem almost like a
castle protecting us from the enemy.

We took turns sitting in a corner, pointing out the guard's position like the hand on a clock, to warn the others in the cell who were talking or moving around.

Inside the castle, common experiences brought us closer to each other. We talked over our deepest problems like brothers.

Even the unbearable weariness of hopeless waiting was lessened by lectures on Esperanto and Japanese.

I invented a pleasingly simple way of singing, so that I could hear my own voice and yet never be heard by the guard.

We succeeded in playing checkers with black and white pel-
lets of hardened rice and a handkerchief checkered by pull-
ing out threads.

Prisoners who came back from investigation smuggled in whatever they could, with the simplicity and bravery of primitive men who brought back animals to their families.

Once I got a quarter-inch square of cheese. I had never had any other experience like it: my whole body trembled while the cheese went humming down to my stomach.

Smuggled books were divided into small sections and de-
voured greedily like food, and when they had been read by
everyone they were reduced to powder and dropped into the
toilet.

After a prisoner who had been a pickpocket was made janitor, the circulation of leftover food was smooth and wasteless.

It became a custom, when a prisoner was very severely tortured, to give him the best part of our lunch — the only encouragement we could offer.

One puff at a time, we even managed to smoke every day.
Sandpaper was stuck permanently under a wooden beam,
match-heads were kept inside shirt labels, and cigarettes
were hidden in the waist hem of our trousers.

A sushi seller in jail for a few weeks was surprised at our
devotion to each other, and he pretended to serve us sushi
patties made of handkerchiefs instead of rice and fish.

When prisoners with short sentences were freed, they almost always took off their own shirts or coats and gave them to the others as a symbol of their thanks.

Even a Korean dope fiend threw in his cigarettes and matches
when he left, in spite of the danger.

The janitor was a good postman, and helped all the prisoners
in the jail keep in touch with each other.

At last the committee which we had chosen to take charge of our cell decided to circulate a news bulletin. Above all, it was necessary to unify all prisoners on some action to be taken in the new year.

The paper-handkerchief bulletin went from one cell to another. "Now with the whole country fighting a war abroad,
it is a great mistake for us who are against it to be separated
over small differences in abstract words."

Part 14

ONE BOTTLE OF MILK

The committee of our cell became skillful and more active.
It made the downfall of the poet guard a common aim.

Since the safety motto I had written for this lout had won a
contest in the police magazine, I became an adviser to his
poetry-making.

Also I did as he wished and drew a caricature of his face;
I was allowed to buy a laxative as payment for it.

A fortune teller among us managed to get medicine for decayed teeth by continually predicting a happy future for the guard.

Permission to cut nails and rub down our bodies was ob-
tained by strategy, and some men with good records won
the privilege of going in and out of their cells without
examination.

But bad luck returned to our cell: an organizer for the city trolley union became very sick and could eat nothing for more than a week. The committee decided upon an emergency plan.

Men who were writing their personal histories complained
to the Tokkoka that the trolley worker would surely die.

Dr. Yama spent the noon toilet time talking gloomily to the
guard. "The man can't possibly go on for more than a few
days."

That same afternoon the sick man pretended to be dying, and the rest of us buzzed like wasps when their nest is disturbed. "Look here, he'll be dead soon!"

When the Tokkoka finally came, Dr. Yama said bitterly, "Of course he had nothing to nourish him. There is only one thing to do — give him milk from now on."

It was almost too much to hope for . . . but at suppertime a
whole bottle of milk appeared in the food opening.

You, sick man, on the point of death, don't drink the whole bottle at once or your fraud will be detected.

The trolley worker took just one mouthful, and could not swallow a second. He was sobbing . . . "Thank you, everybody, thank you."

In the middle of that night, I saw him, still excited, writing
a poem on the wall. The feeling of friendship in our cell
was so complete that I thought to myself, perhaps this is a
sample of the future world.

Part 15

PEOPLE OF TOMORROW

When spring came, the shapes of many people I had known
bloomed inside me one by one like the flowers that raised
their heads out of the earth.

Once more I wanted to talk to the farmer who had told me that he would like to be painted standing on top of a rock with his plow.

I wondered about the health of the old man who owned not
a foot of land but who had said, "When you work on me I
look like a premier, in the painting, don't I?"

And that poor young farmer who wanted to go to the city
and earn enough money to buy books. . . . Had he been able
to leave his village?

Another friend of whom I thought was a boy who hated his
drunkard father but dreamed of becoming a sign-painter in
order to help his hard-working mother.

What had happened to the mind of the farmer who became strangely quiet and unlike himself after he had killed a pleading mother and child in the Manchurian war?

I wondered whether the maid who was working like a squir-
rel to bring her boy up to be a skillful machine worker, like
her dead husband, would still be in the same lunch store?

Would the mechanic who once asked my advice about his brother's artistic talent still be assembling engines?

What were the Korean children looking around for now, the ones who had divided a piece of tinfoil exactly in half because they found it at exactly the same time?

Had recognition come to the young writer I had known who barely kept himself alive by cleaning streets one or two days a week in order to write about the things he could not forget?

I longed for the stuffed rice-cakes of the old peddler who was taking care of his little boy like a mother after his wife's death.

What were the thoughts, now, of the dockyard lathe operator who had tried, with nothing but gestures, to ask a German sailor about the German people's situation?

I remembered the workers' wives who had sympathetically watched the funeral of a Russian sailor accidentally killed when his boat was in dock. Had they troubles of their own by this time?

What would the miner contributor to our picture magazine be drawing? Long ago he had written me that he was pushing a coal car in the daytime and at night making a portrait of his brother who had died in the Manchurian war.

One idea was being forced upon all these working people:
To Kill the other nations for the "Peace of the East."

Whose peace on earth would it be when that peace was made by forcing working people to use their hands to kill other working people?

Horrible sacrifice awaited these people. . . . But finally,
through hunger, sickness, and death, they would learn to
build a people's Japan, a people's Orient!

With the committee, I made up my mind about the "confession" the Tokkoka wanted from me. It would be a practical way to get out and work with the people instead of impotently proclaiming their right to the cultural movement.

Part 16

THE NEW SUN

A month and a half passed after I finished my second personal history before I was called by the Tokkoka.

As I expected, I was to be permitted to go free. "But there's a rope tied around your neck," the chief added.

And there, on top of the chief's desk, was an undelivered
telegram for me: my wife had safely borne a healthy baby
boy!

After the farewells to my cellmates, I left the prison, and
as I stepped through the gates, the air of spring enveloped
me.

Light overflowed the street and a trolley car squeaked by, swinging the people inside.

I did not want to eat any of the food I had planned for in
such variety.

Casually I stepped into a secondhand book store. A print of
the Virgin Saskia dedicating a flower to Rembrandt was
waiting for me.

I passed by our old house. A poppy we had planted was a bright red flower now.

Farther on, my feet took me toward a hill I had once
sketched.

Factory chimneys were puffing out great streams of smoke.
I could feel the rhythm of labor in my body.

A train was running toward the house of my wife's parents. There my new baby would by lying—breathing. The sun was shining above me, big and bright.

Surely this new sun would increase its brightness over me and over all people everywhere.